George Washington
1st U.S. President

Beginner
Biographies

written by M. J. Cosson   illustrated by Reed Sprunger

Content Consultant:
Richard Jensen, PhD
Author, Scholar, and Historian

magic
wagon

visit us at www.abdopublishing.com

Published by Magic Wagon, a division of the ABDO Publishing Group, 8000 West 78th Street, Edina, Minnesota 55439. Copyright © 2009 by Abdo Consulting Group, Inc. International copyrights reserved in all countries. All rights reserved. No part of this book may be reproduced in any form without written permission from the publisher.

Looking Glass Library™ is a trademark and logo of Magic Wagon.

Printed in the United States.

Text by M. J. Cosson
Illustrations by Reed Sprunger
Edited by Nadia Higgins
Interior layout and design by Emily Love
Cover design by Emily Love

Library of Congress Cataloging-in-Publication Data

Cosson, M. J.
  George Washington : 1st U.S. president / by M.J. Cosson ; illustrated by Reed Sprunger.
    p. cm. — (Beginner biographies)
  Includes index.
  ISBN 978-1-60270-253-0
  1. Washington, George, 1732-1799—Juvenile literature. 2. Presidents—United States–Biography–Juvenile literature. I. Sprunger, Reed, ill. II. Title.
  E312.66.C67 2009
  973.4'1092–dc22
  [B]
                              2008002891

Table of Contents

Growing Up on the Farm

George Washington was born on February 22, 1732. As a boy, he lived in the colony of Virginia. Virginia was not a state yet. At the time, there were no states, just colonies.

England had power over all the colonies. George's family had come from England. They were loyal to the king of England.

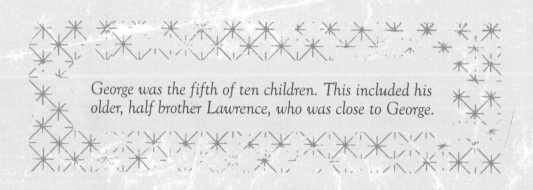

George was the fifth of ten children. This included his older, half brother Lawrence, who was close to George.

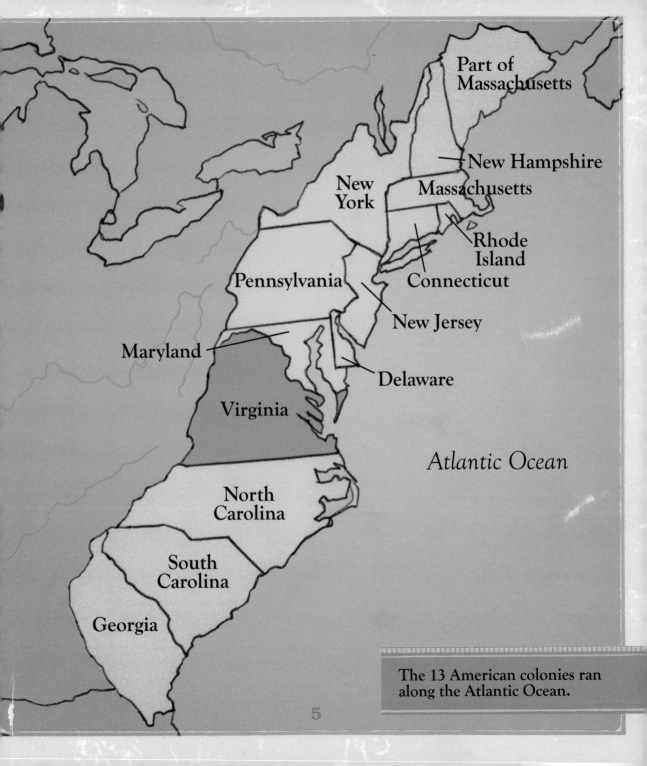

Part of
Massachusetts

New Hampshire

New
York

Massachusetts

Rhode
Island

Pennsylvania

Connecticut

New Jersey

Maryland

Delaware

Virginia

Atlantic Ocean

North
Carolina

South
Carolina

Georgia

The 13 American colonies ran
along the Atlantic Ocean.

George's father owned a large farm. George had to do many chores. He also played with his brothers and sisters in the woods nearby.

George was homeschooled by his father and his brother Lawrence. Many children did not get to go to school at that time. George studied hard. His favorite subject was math.

Young George liked to
play on his family farm.

The house at Mount Vernon
is a beautiful mansion.

When George was 11, his father died. George was the oldest child at home. He helped his mother with the farm.

As a teenager, George often visited Lawrence. George's older brother lived in a big house on a farm. The estate was called Mount Vernon.

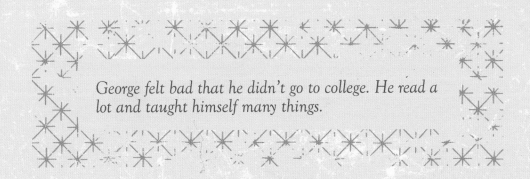

George felt bad that he didn't go to college. He read a lot and taught himself many things.

Teenage Years

George loved Mount Vernon. There, Lawrence told George thrilling war stories. The stories were about Lawrence's own time as a soldier.

Lawrence decided that George should join the navy. Being a sailor sounded exciting to George. But George's mother said no.

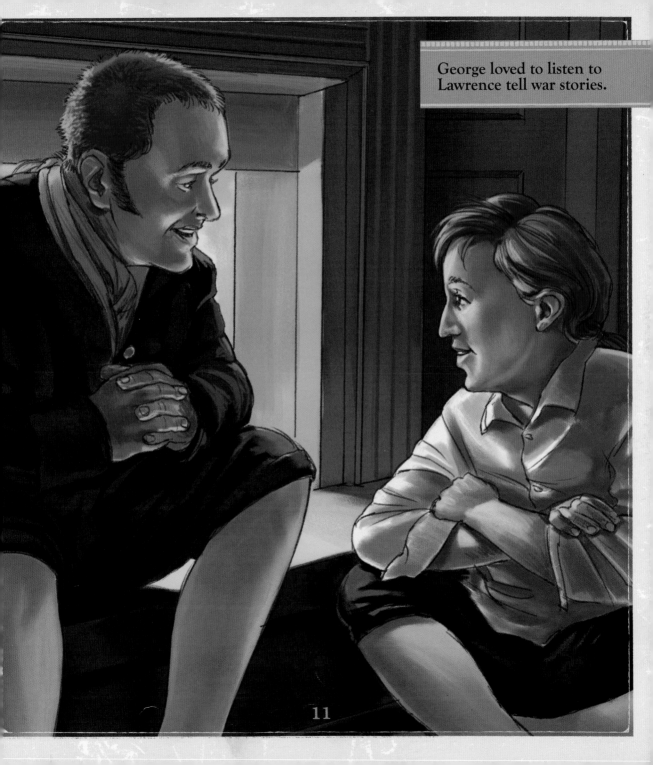

George loved to listen to Lawrence tell war stories.

11

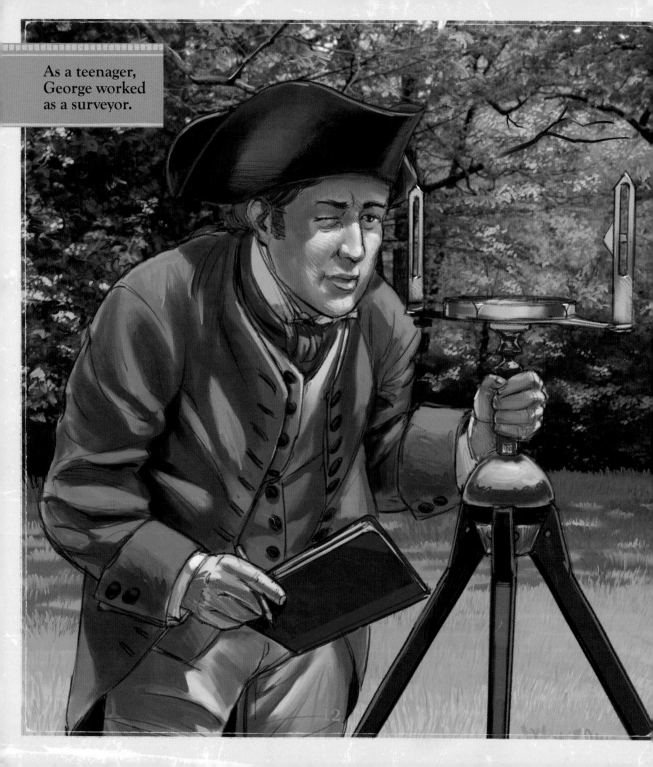

As a teenager,
George worked
as a surveyor.

At 16, George became a surveyor instead. His job was to mark out new farms in the wilderness. George liked exploring the frontier. He was paid well for his work.

When George was 20, Lawrence died. Mount Vernon would soon belong to George.

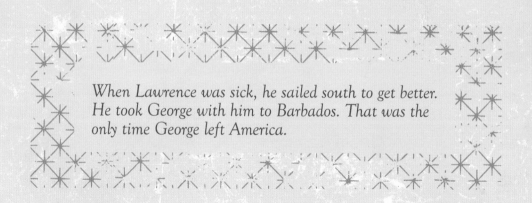

When Lawrence was sick, he sailed south to get better. He took George with him to Barbados. That was the only time George left America.

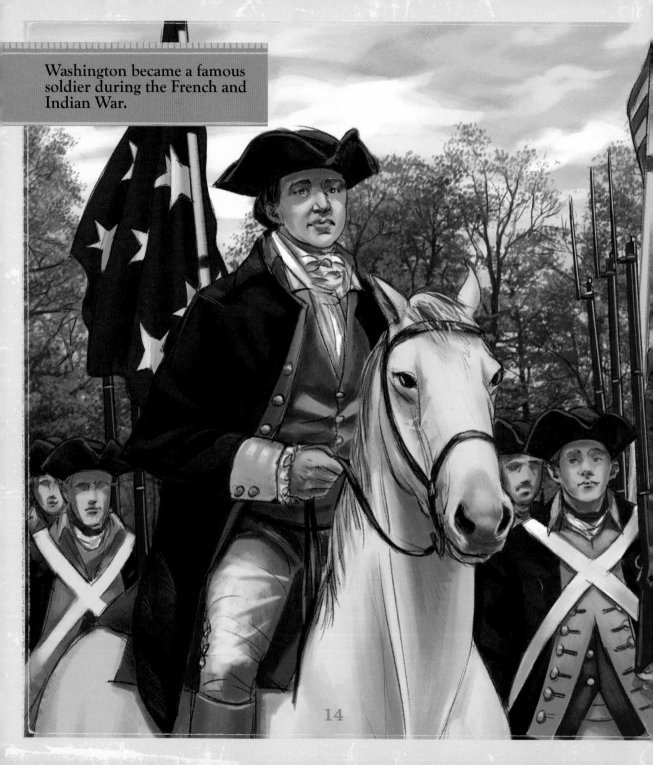

Washington became a famous soldier during the French and Indian War.

The Beginnings of a Soldier

In 1753, England and France were enemies. The two countries fought over land near the American colonies. Some Indians sided with the French.

George Washington fought against the French and the Indians. He wanted to protect the colonies. He was a good leader, and his men liked him. By the end of the war, Washington was a colonel in the army.

Life in Virginia

After the war, Washington went home to Mount Vernon. He took care of his house and crops. He helped write many new laws. The people of Virginia liked him.

Soon, George Washington met Martha Custis. They got married in 1759. George and Martha lived a quiet life at Mount Vernon.

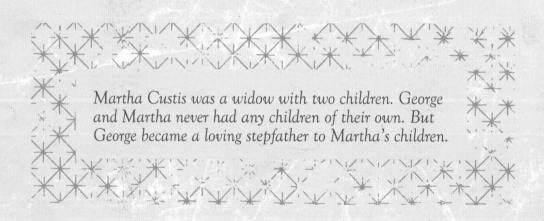

Martha Custis was a widow with two children. George and Martha never had any children of their own. But George became a loving stepfather to Martha's children.

Washington married
Martha Custis.

Meanwhile, the colonists were growing tired of British rule. Britain was making them pay taxes. But the colonists had no say in running the government. The colonists held meetings about what to do. They asked Washington for advice. He did not think the taxes were fair.

In 1774, the First Continental Congress of the colonies met. Washington was one of seven men from Virginia. The Congress decided to shut off trade with Britain.

American colonists listened carefully to what Washington said about the British.

Washington led the fight against the British.

Army Commander

Soon, the colonists decided that they did not want to be under British rule anymore. They set up their own government. They called the colonies the United States of America.

The British did not want the colonists to be on their own. The colonists formed an army. They made Washington the leader of the army.

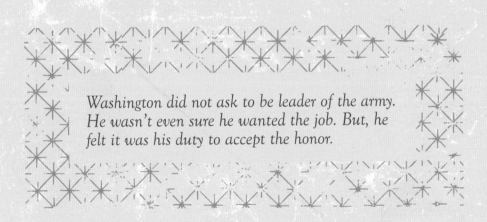

Washington did not ask to be leader of the army. He wasn't even sure he wanted the job. But, he felt it was his duty to accept the honor.

Washington's brave leadership made him an American hero.

The American Revolutionary War lasted eight years. During this time, Washington's men faced many problems. Washington met the problems with courage and determination. The American people looked to Washington for hope. He became a hero.

Then the French joined the war. They fought on the side of the Americans. At last in 1781, French and American forces captured the main British army at Yorktown, Virginia. By 1783, the war was over. The Americans had won their freedom from England!

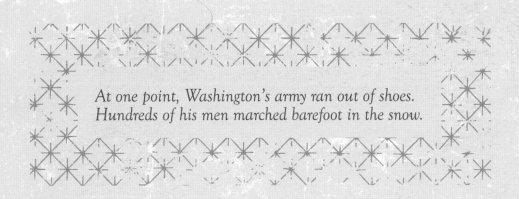

At one point, Washington's army ran out of shoes. Hundreds of his men marched barefoot in the snow.

President Washington

Some army officers said Washington should be made king of the new country. But, Washington did not want the kind of government that had a king.

At the time, the United States had many problems. It needed a strong leader. In 1789, Washington was elected president of the United States.

Washington was sworn in as the first U.S. president.

Today, the White House is a famous landmark of Washington, D.C.

26

Washington was an honest leader. He worked with Congress and didn't try to be too powerful. He set an example for future U.S. presidents.

Washington served two terms. Many people asked him to stay on for a third term. Washington was 64 years old and ready to step aside. He said no.

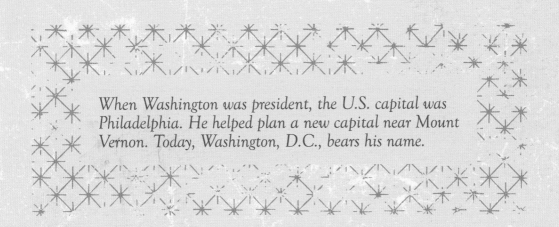

When Washington was president, the U.S. capital was Philadelphia. He helped plan a new capital near Mount Vernon. Today, Washington, D.C., bears his name.

Final Years

Washington happily returned to Mount Vernon with Martha. He continued to give advice about running the country. He wrote many letters and had visitors almost every day. On December 14, 1799, Washington woke up sick. He died later that night.

Today, Americans remember their first president in many ways. In the capital, the giant Washington Monument towers over the city. It honors the man who helped create the United States of America.

The Washington Monument was built in honor of George Washington.

FUN FACTS

✦ Not much is known about George Washington's childhood. So some writers made up stories. One person said George chopped down a cherry tree. When his father asked him if he did it, George said yes. He said he could not tell a lie. George was a good man, but this story is not true.

✦ Washington was 6 feet 2 inches (1.9 m) tall. He was taller than most men of that time.

✦ Washington didn't talk much. He had good manners and only spoke when he needed to. People admired him for that.

✦ Washington was the only president who didn't live in the White House. It wasn't built yet.

TIMELINE

1732 George Washington was born on February 22.

1753–1758 Washington earned fame as a colonel during the French and Indian War.

1759 Washington married Martha Custis on January 6.

1774 Washington met with colonial leaders at the First Continental Congress in September.

1775–1783 Washington led Americans to victory during the American Revolutionary War.

1789–1797 Washington served as the first U.S. president.

1799 Washington died on December 14.

GLOSSARY

American Revolutionary War—the war, from 1775 to 1783, in which the American colonists gained freedom from British rule.

capital—the city where the president and other national leaders live and work.

colonel—an important officer in the army.

colony—a place ruled by another country. The United States began as 13 colonies ruled by Britain.

Congress—the group that makes laws for the United States.

elect—to choose a leader by voting.

frontier—the border between settled land and wilderness.

surveyor—someone who measures land.

taxes—money a government makes people pay to help run the government.

LEARN MORE

At the Library

Adler, David. *President George Washington*. New York: Holiday House, 2005.

Devillier, Christy. *George Washington*. First Biographies. Edina: ABDO Publishing Company, 2001.

Peacock, Louise. *Crossing the Delaware: A History in Many Voices*. New York: Aladdin, 2007.

Venezia, Mike. *George Washington: First President*. New York: Children's Press, 2004.

On the Web

To learn more about George Washington, visit ABDO Publishing Company on the World Wide Web at **www.abdopublishing.com**. Web sites about Washington are featured on our Book Links page. These links are routinely monitored and updated to provide the most current information available.

INDEX